Vintage Prints Constellations, Zodiac, and Star Charts

All rights reserved. This book, or parts thereof, may not be reproduced in any form without permission. Images found in this book may have been retouched.

PLATE A.
THE CONSTELLATIONS SURROUNDING THE NORTH POLE.
ALWAYS VISIBLE IN THE NORTHERN HEMISPHERE.

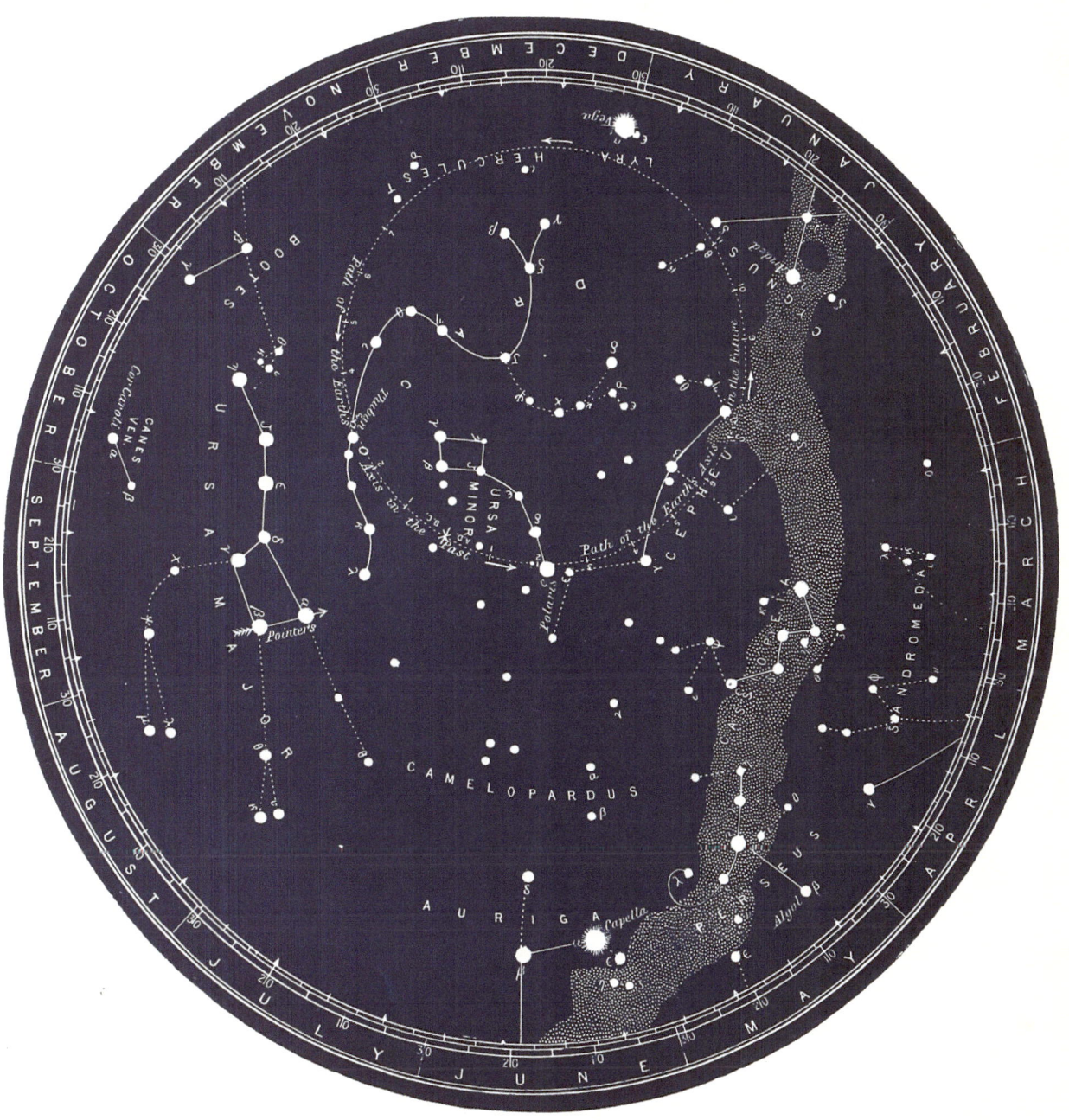

THE above Map is a representation of the Starry Heavens near the North Pole. These Stars are always to be seen on every clear night, as they never sink below our Northern Horizon, but appear to revolve round the Pole in the same time that the Earth takes to rotate on its axis, and in an opposite direction from the hands of a watch.

For a description of this Map, and the manner of using it see page 11.

PLATE B.
THE CONSTELLATIONS SURROUNDING THE SOUTH POLE.
NEVER VISIBLE IN THE NORTHERN HEMISPHERE.

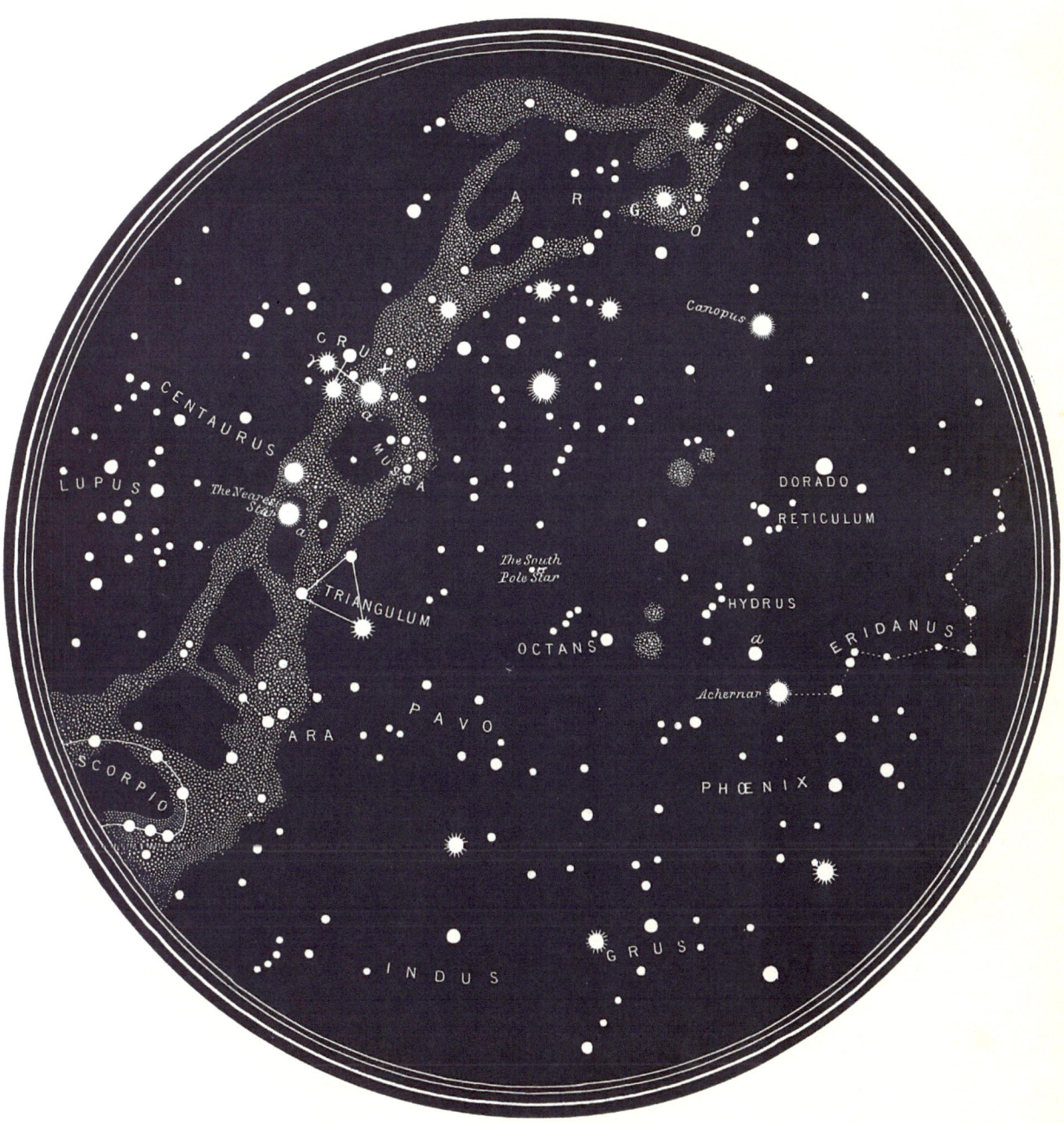

THE above Map is a representation of the Starry Heavens near the South Pole. These Stars are not seen in Britain, as they never appear above our Southern Horizon.

For a description of this part of the Heavens see page 13.

MAP I.
THE CONSTELLATIONS FOR OCTOBER AND NOVEMBER.

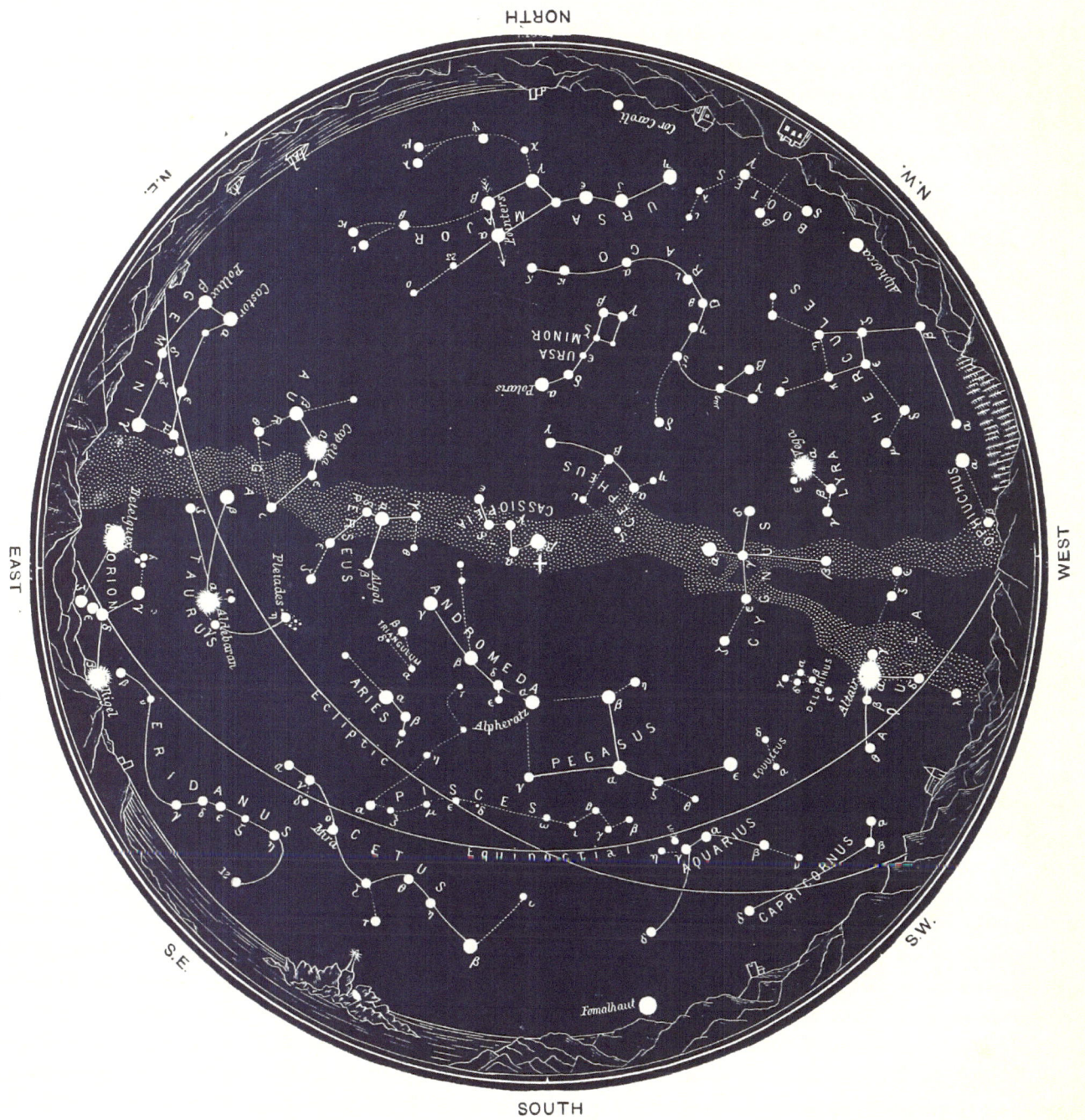

The above Map is a representation of the Starry Heavens in the Evening at the following Dates and Hours:—

OCTOBER	16 at	...	...	10.20	NOVEMBER	6 at	...	...	9.0	NOVEMBER	26 at	...	...	7.40
	21 ,,	...	...	10.0		11 ,,	...	...	8.40	DECEMBER	1 ,,	...	...	7.20
	26 ,,	...	...	9.40		16 ,,	...	...	8.20		6 ,,	...	...	7.0
	31 ,,	...	...	9.20		21 ,,	...	...	8.0		11 ,,	...	...	6.40

The circular boundary of this Map represents the Horizon, with the principal points of the compass indicated. The Cross in the centre is the zenith or that part of the sky which is directly overhead.

A list of Arabic names of the Principal Stars corresponding to the Greek letters in each Constellation is given on page 16.

MAP II.
THE CONSTELLATIONS FOR NOVEMBER AND DECEMBER.

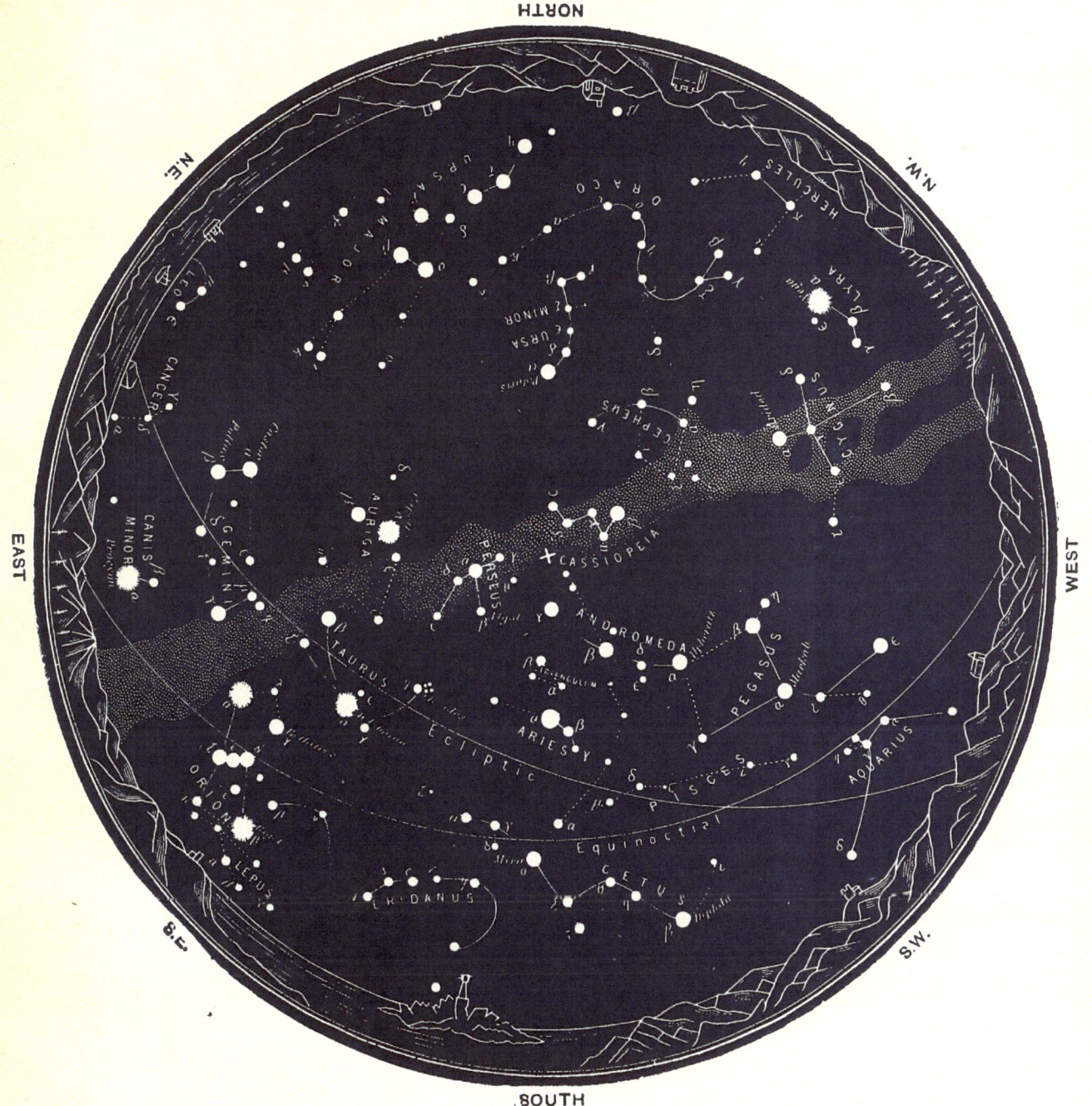

The above Map is a representation of the Starry Heavens in the Evening at the following Dates and Hours:—

NOVEMBER 16 at … … 10.20	DECEMBER 6 at … … 9.0	DECEMBER 26 at … … 7.40
21 ,, … … 10.0	11 ,, … … 8.40	31 ,, … … 7.20
26 ,, … … 9.40	16 ,, … … 8.20	JANUARY 5 ,, … … 7.0
DECEMBER 1 ,, … … 9.20	21 ,, … … 8.0	10 ,, … … 6.40

The circular boundary of this Map represents the Horizon, with the principal points of the compass indicated. The Cross in the centre is the zenith or that part of the sky which is directly overhead.

A list of Arabic names of the Principal Stars corresponding to the Greek letters in each Constellation is given on page 16.

MAP III.
THE CONSTELLATIONS FOR DECEMBER AND JANUARY.

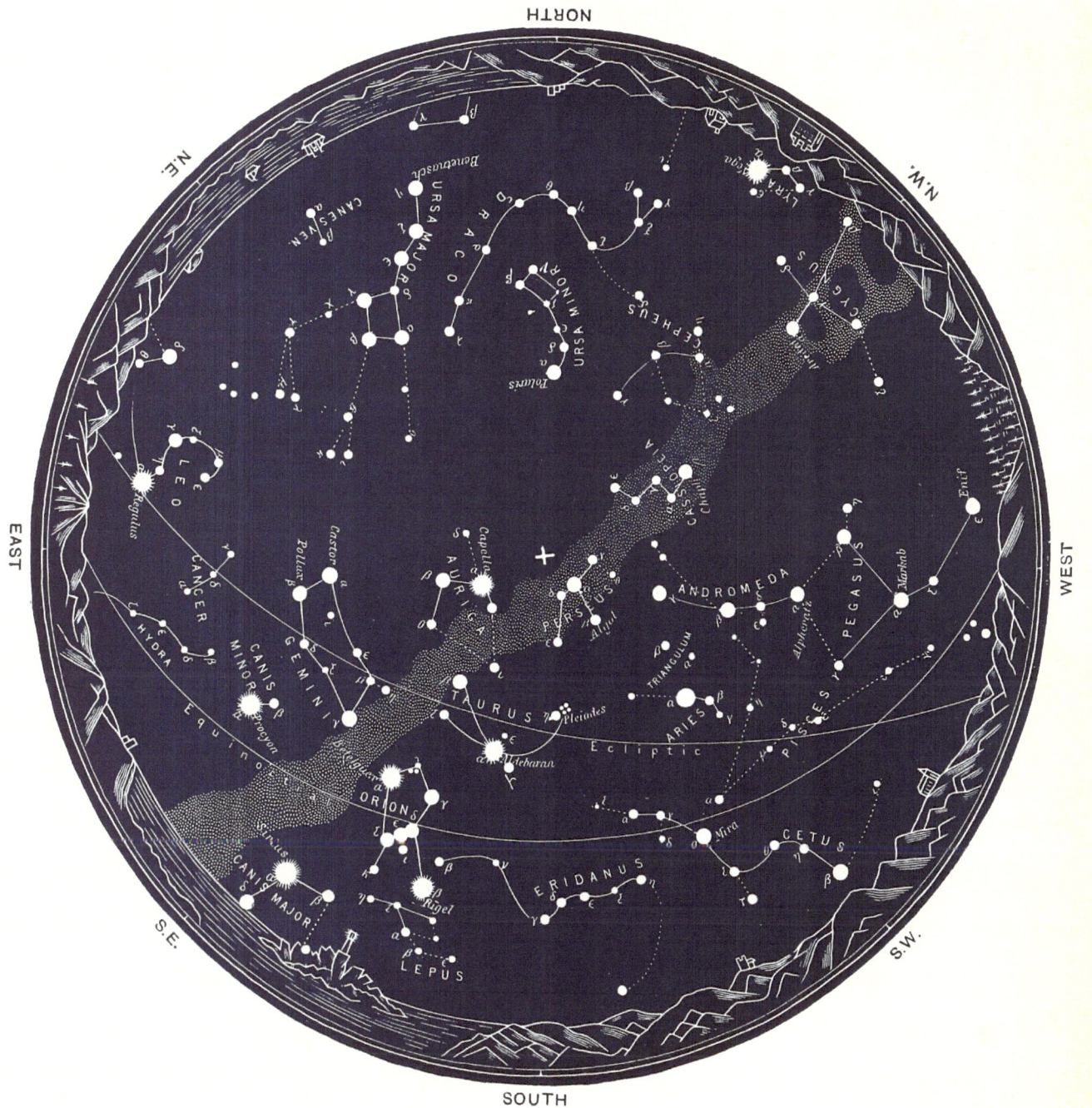

The above Map is a representation of the Starry Heavens in the Evening at the following Dates and Hours :—

DECEMBER	16 at	...	...	10.20	JANUARY	5 at	...	...	9.0	JANUARY	25 at	...	...	7.40
	21 ,,	...	...	10.0		10 ,,	...	...	8.40		30 ,,	...	...	7.20
	26 ,,	...	...	9.40		15 ,,	...	...	8.20	FEBRUARY	5 ,,	...	...	7.0
	31 ,,	...	...	9.20		20 ,,	...	...	8.0		10 ,,	...	...	6.40

The circular boundary of this Map represents the Horizon, with the principal points of the compass indicated. The Cross in the centre is the zenith or that part of the sky which is directly overhead.

A list of Arabic names of the Principal Stars corresponding to the Greek letters in each Constellation is given on page 16.

MAP IV.

THE CONSTELLATIONS FOR JANUARY AND FEBRUARY

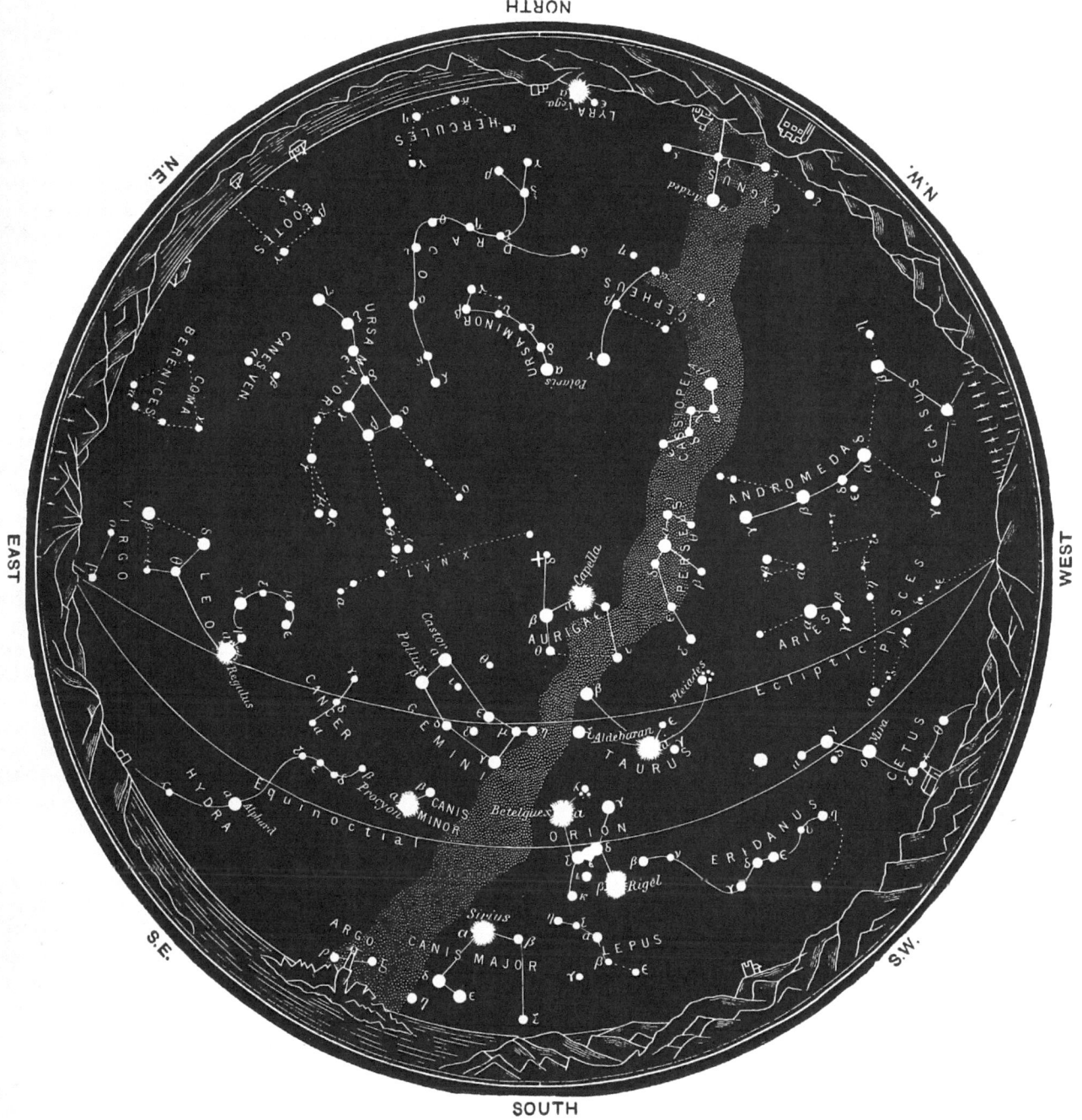

The above Map is a representation of the Starry Heavens in the Evening at the following Dates and Hours :—

JANUARY	15 at	...	...	10.20	FEBRUARY	5 at	...	...	9.0	FEBRUARY	25 at	...	...	7.40
	20 ,,	...	...	10.0		10 ,,	...	...	8.40	MARCH	2 ,,	...	...	7.20
	25 ,,	...	...	9.40		15 ,,	...	...	8.20		7 ,,	...	...	7.0
	30 ,,	...	...	9.20		20 ,,	...	...	8.0		12 ,,	...	...	6.40

The circular boundary of this Map represents the Horizon, with the principal points of the compass indicated. The Cross in the centre is the zenith or that part of the sky which is directly overhead.

A list of Arabic names of the Principal Stars corresponding to the Greek letters in each Constellation is given on page 16.

MAP V.
THE CONSTELLATIONS FOR FEBRUARY AND MARCH

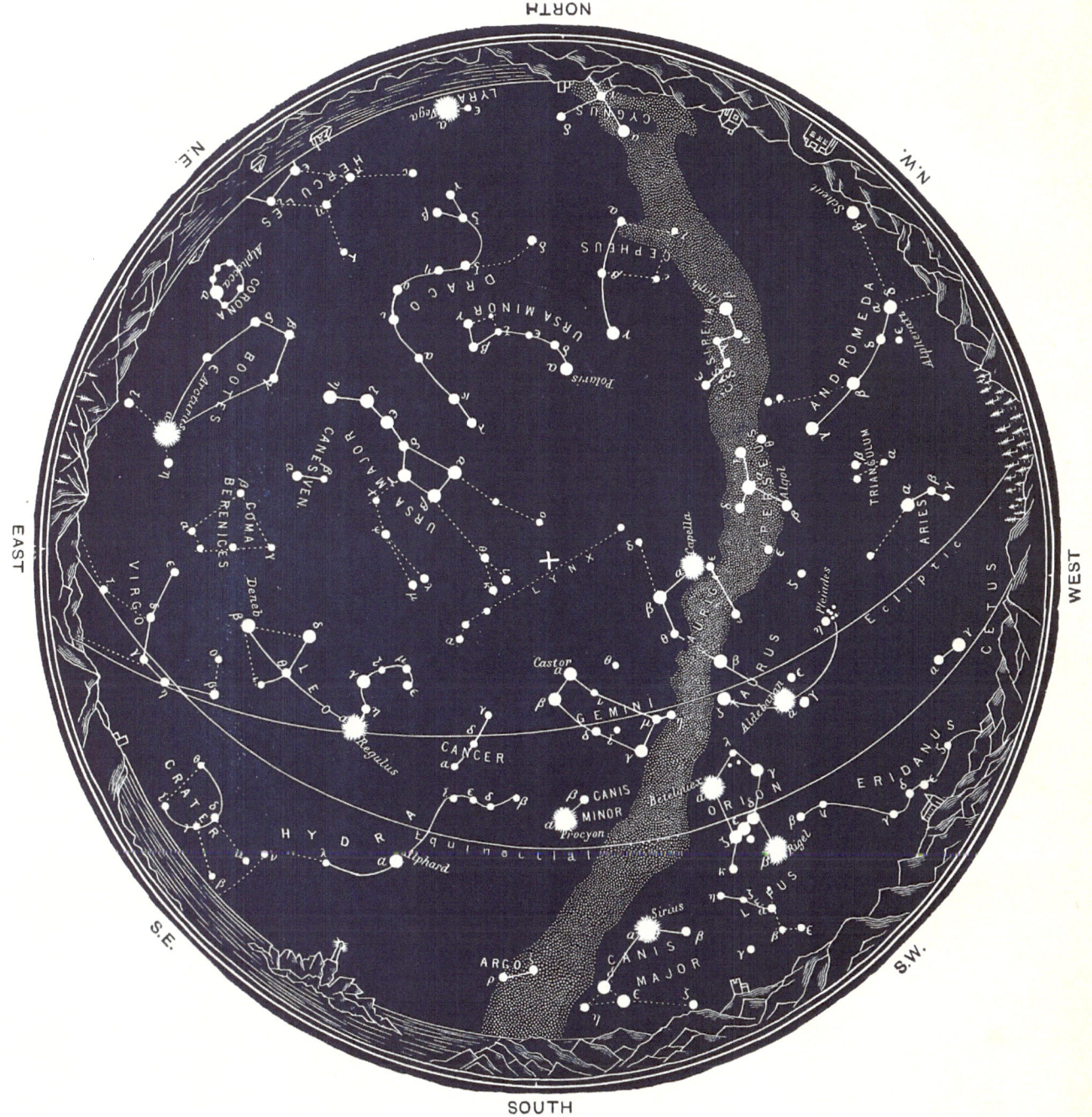

The above Map is a representation of the Starry Heavens in the Evening at the following Dates and Hours:—

FEBRUARY	15 at	...	...	10.20	MARCH	7 at	...	...	9.0	MARCH	27 at	...	...	7.40
	20 ,,	...	...	10.0		12 ,,	...	...	8.40	APRIL	1 ,,	...	...	7.20
	25 ,,	...	...	9.40		17 ,,	...	...	8.20		6 ,,	...	...	7.0
MARCH	2 ,,	...	...	9.20		22 ,,	...	...	8.0		11 ,,	...	...	6.40

The circular boundary of this Map represents the Horizon, with the principal points of the compass indicated. The Cross in the centre is the zenith or that part of the sky which is directly overhead.

A list of Arabic names of the Principal Stars corresponding to the Greek letters in each Constellation is given on page 16.

MAP VI.

THE CONSTELLATIONS FOR MARCH AND APRIL.

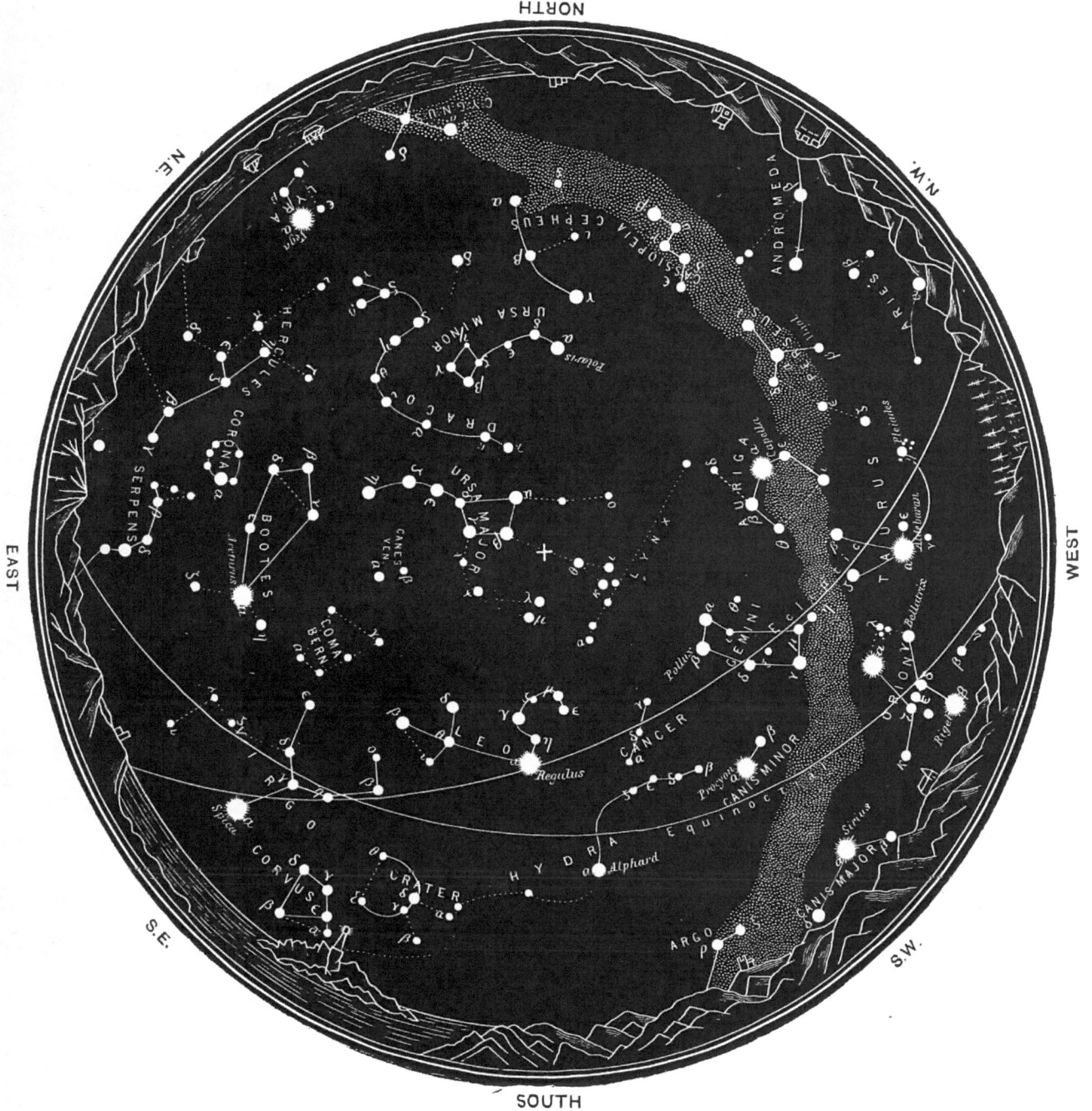

The above Map is a representation of the Starry Heavens in the Evening at the following Dates and Hours :—

MARCH	7 at	...	...	11.0	MARCH	27 at	...	...	9.40	APRIL	16 at	...	...	8.20
	12 ,,	...	...	10.40	APRIL	1 ,,	...	...	9.20		21 ,,	...	...	8.0
	17 ,,	...	...	10.20		6 ,,	...	...	9.0		26 ,,	...	...	7.40
	22 ,,	...	...	10.0		11 ,,	...	...	8.40	MAY	2 ,,	...	...	7.20

The circular boundary of this Map represents the Horizon, with the principal points of the compass indicated. The Cross in the centre is the zenith or that part of the sky which is directly overhead.

A list of Arabic names of the Principal Stars corresponding to the Greek letters in each Constellation is given on page 16.

MAP VII.

THE CONSTELLATIONS FOR APRIL AND MAY.

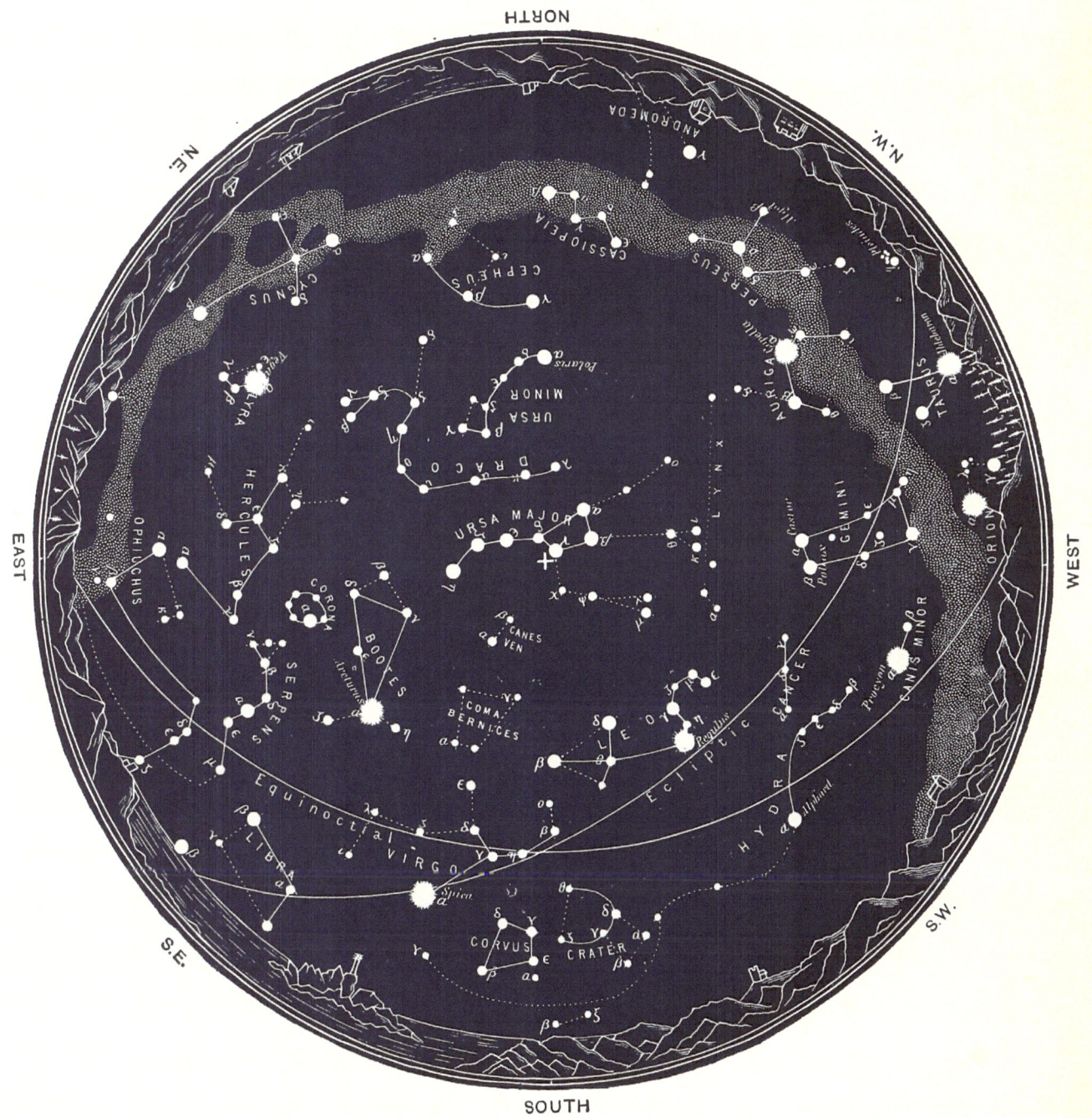

The above Map is a representation of the Starry Heavens in the Evening at the following Dates and Hours:—

APRIL	6 at	...	...	11.0	APRIL	21 at	...	...	10.0	MAY	7 at	...	...	9.0
	11 „	...	...	10.40		26 „	...	...	9.40		12 „	...	...	8.40
	16 „	...	...	10.20	MAY	2 „	...	...	9.20		17 „	...	...	8.20

The circular boundary of this Map represents the Horizon, with the principal points of the compass indicated. The Cross in the centre is the zenith or that part of the sky which is directly overhead.

A list of Arabic names of the Principal Stars corresponding to the Greek letters in each Constellation is given on page 16.

MAP VIII.
THE CONSTELLATIONS FOR MAY AND JUNE.

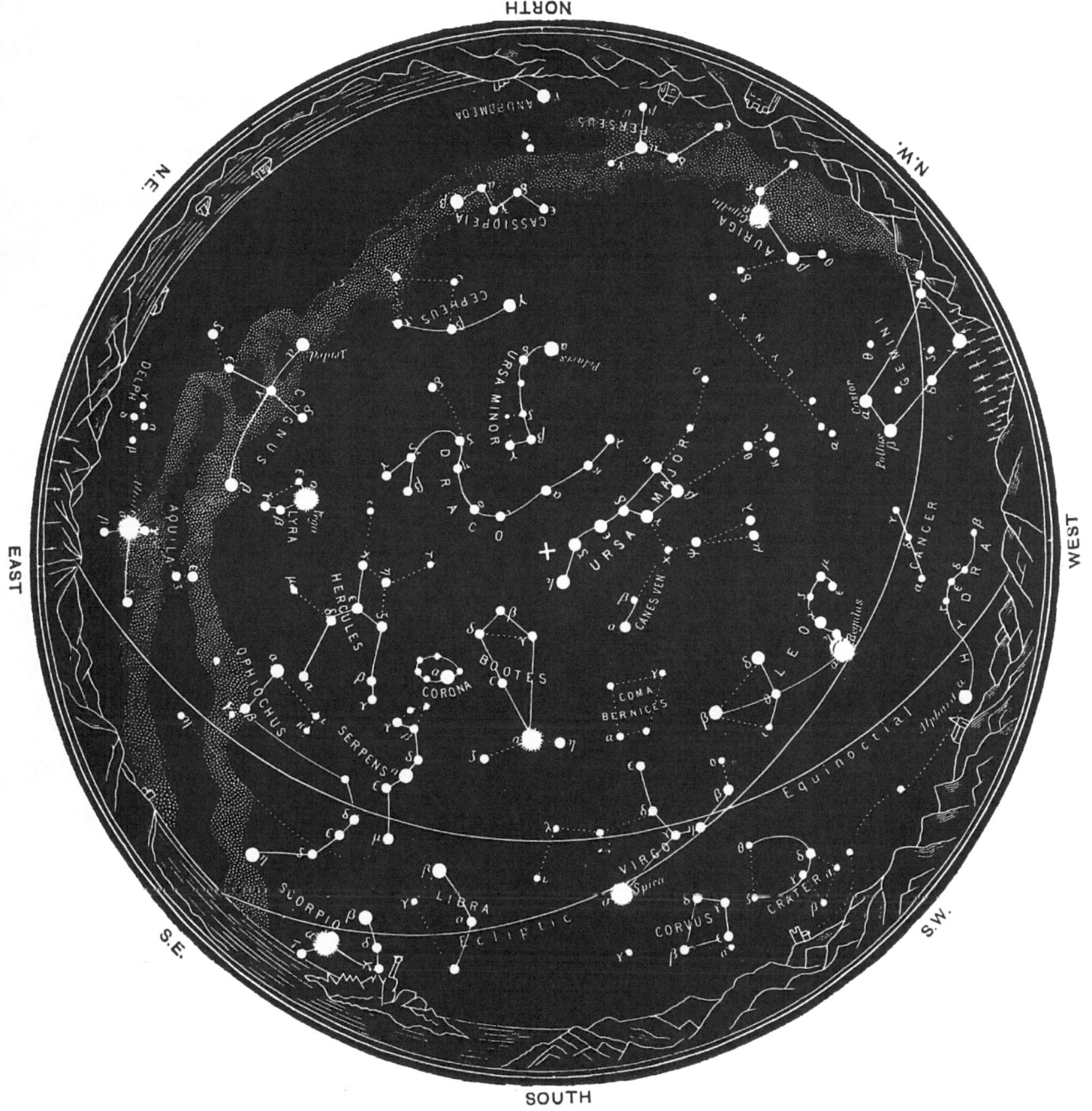

The above Map is a representation of the Starry Heavens in the Evening at the following Dates and Hours:—

MAY	2 at	...	...	11.20	MAY	17 at	...	...	10.20	JUNE	1 at	...	...	9.20
	7 ,,	...	...	11.0		22 ,,	...	...	10.0		6 ,,	...	...	9.0
	12 ,,	...	...	10.40		27 ,,	...	...	9.40		11 ,,	...	...	8.40

The circular boundary of this Map represents the Horizon, with the principal points of the compass indicated. The Cross in the centre is the zenith or that part of the sky which is directly overhead.
A list of Arabic names of the Principal Stars corresponding to the Greek letters in each Constellation is given on page 16.

MAP IX.
THE CONSTELLATIONS FOR JUNE AND JULY.

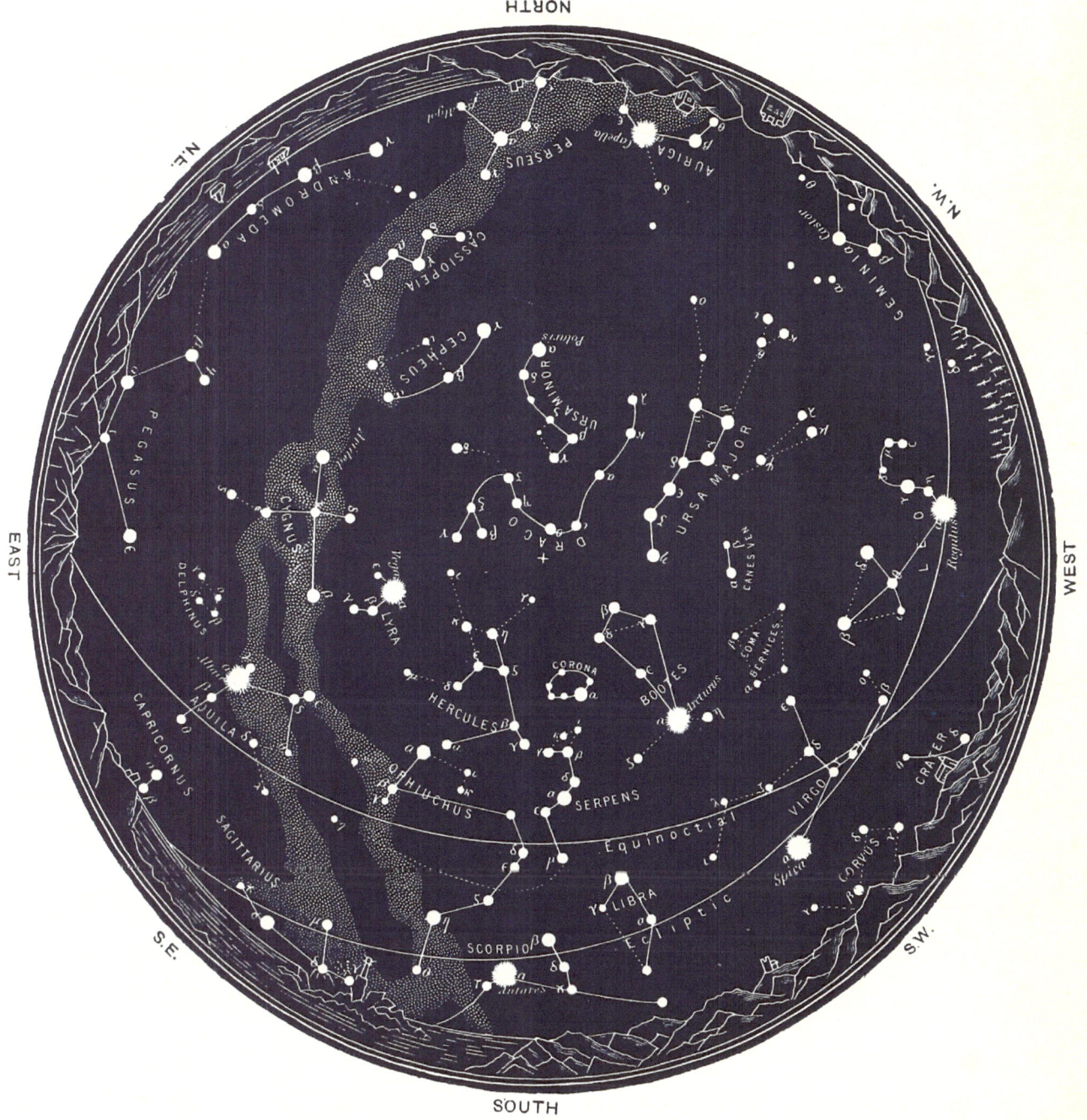

The above Map is a representation of the Starry Heavens in the Evening at the following Dates and Hours:—

JUNE	1 at	...	...	11.20	JUNE	16 at	...	...	10.20	JULY	2 at	...	...	9.20
	6 ,,	...	...	11.0		21 ,,	...	...	10.0		7 ,,	...	...	9.0
	11 ,,	...	...	10.40		26 ,,	..	...	9.40		12 ,,	...	...	8.40

The circular boundary of this Map represents the Horizon, with the principal points of the compass indicated. The Cross in the centre is the zenith or that part of the sky which is directly overhead.
A list of Arabic names of the Principal Stars corresponding to the Greek letters in each Constellation is given on page 16.

MAP X.

THE CONSTELLATIONS FOR JULY AND AUGUST

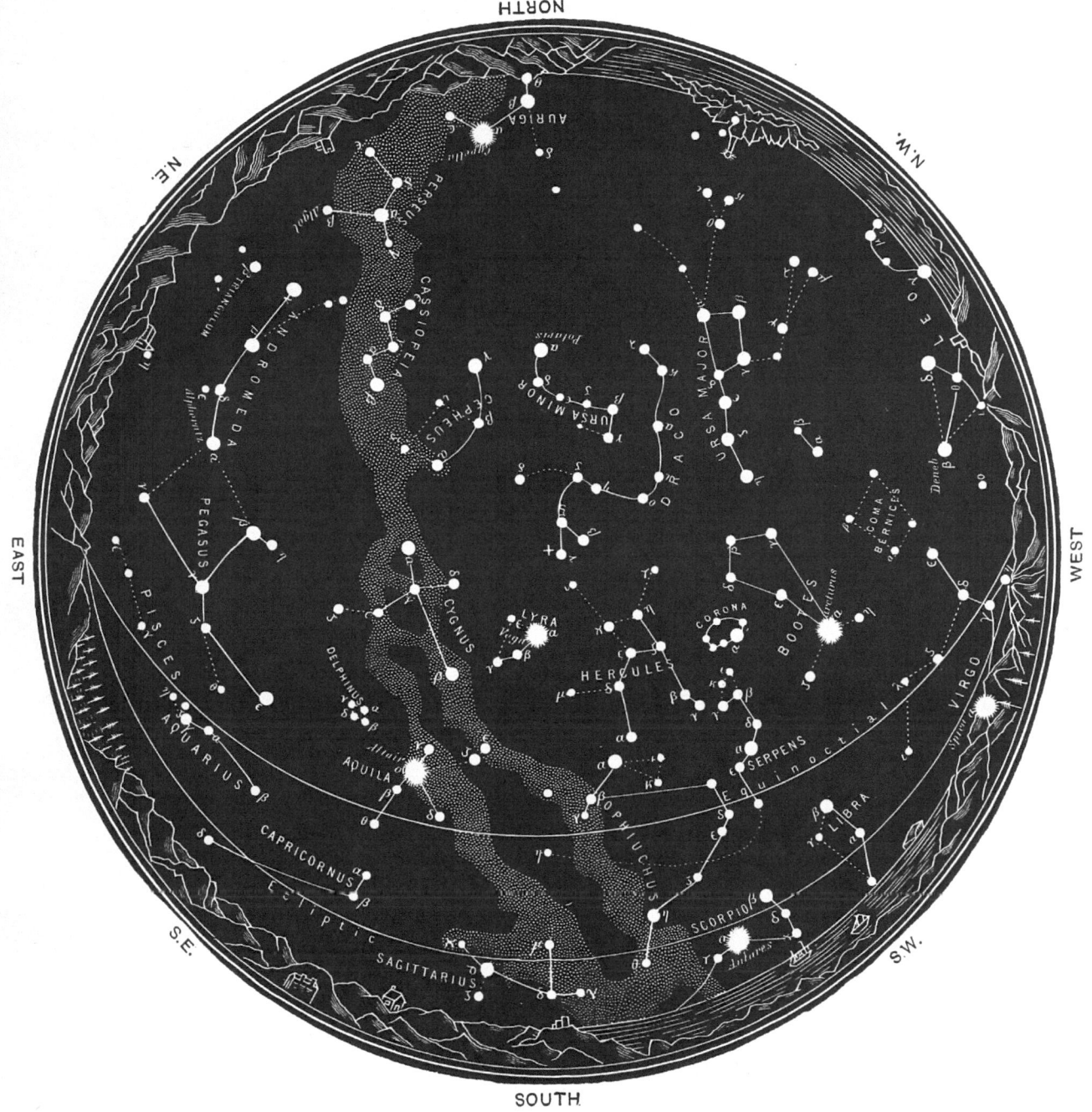

The above Map is a representation of the Starry Heavens in the Evening at the following Dates and Hours:—

JULY	7 at	...	...	11.0	JULY	22 at	...	...	10.0	AUGUST	6 at	...	...	9.0
	12 ,,	...	...	10.40		27 ,,	...	...	9.40		11 ,,	...	...	8.40
	17 ,,	...	...	10.20	AUGUST	1 ,,	...	...	9.20		16 ,,	...	...	8.20

The circular boundary of this Map represents the Horizon, with the principal points of the compass indicated. The Cross in the centre is the zenith or that part of the sky which is directly overhead.

A list of Arabic names of the Principal Stars corresponding to the Greek letters in each Constellation is given on page 16.

MAP XI.
THE CONSTELLATIONS FOR AUGUST AND SEPTEMBER.

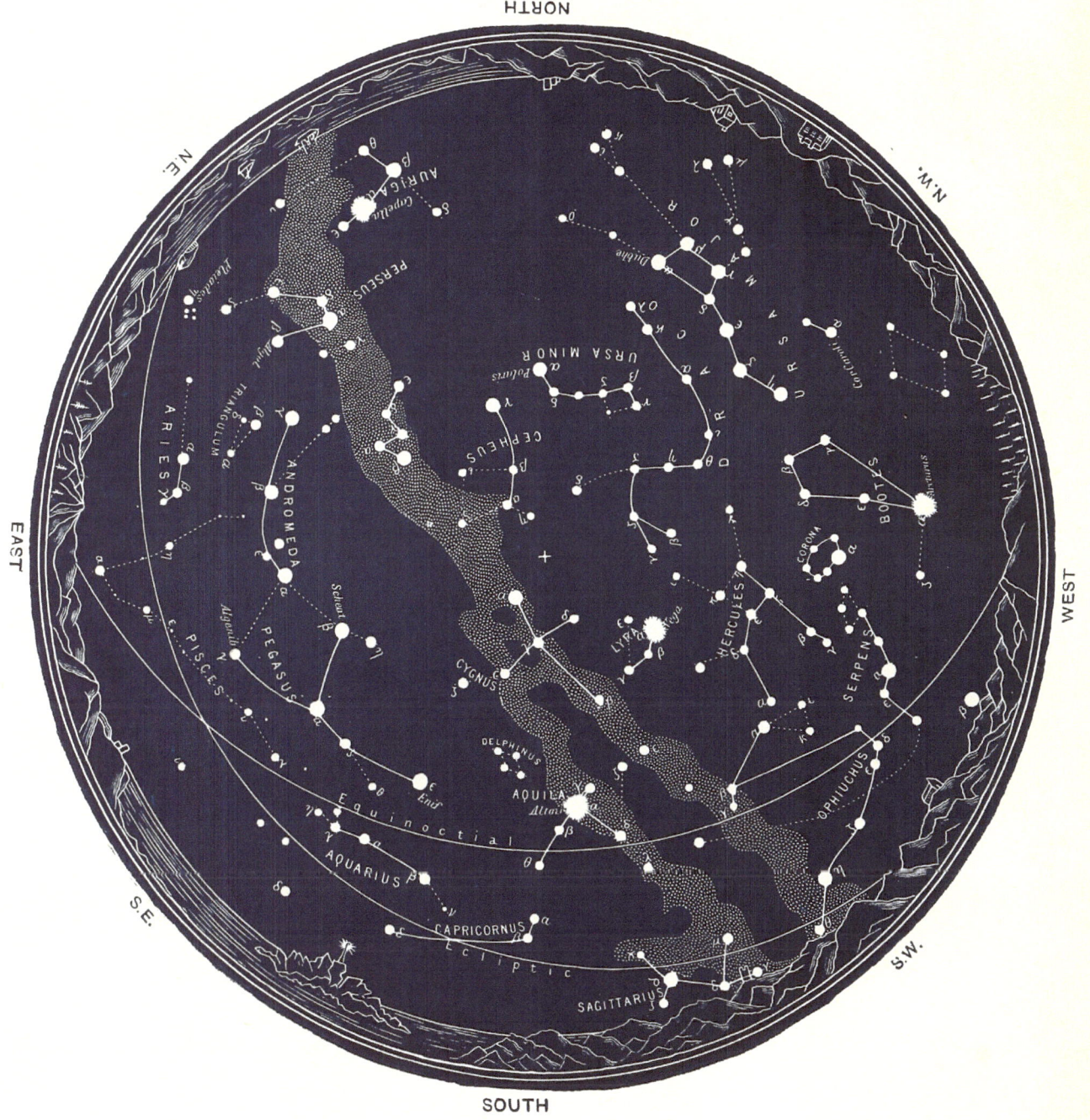

The above Map is a representation of the Starry Heavens in the Evening at the following Dates and Hours :—

August	6 at	...	...	11.0	August	26 at	...	...	9.40	September	16 at	...	...	8.20
	11 ,,	...	...	10.40		31 ,,	...	...	9.20		21 ,,	...	...	8.0
	16 ,,	...	...	10.20	September	6 ,,	...	...	9.0		26 ,,	...	...	7.40
	21 ,,	...	...	10.0		11 ,,	...	...	8.40	October	1 ,,	...	...	7.20

The circular boundary of this Map represents the Horizon, with the principal points of the compass indicated. The Cross in the centre is the zenith or that part of the sky which is directly overhead.

A list of Arabic names of the Principal Stars corresponding to the Greek letters in each Constellation is given on page 16.

MAP XII.
THE CONSTELLATIONS FOR SEPTEMBER AND OCTOBER.

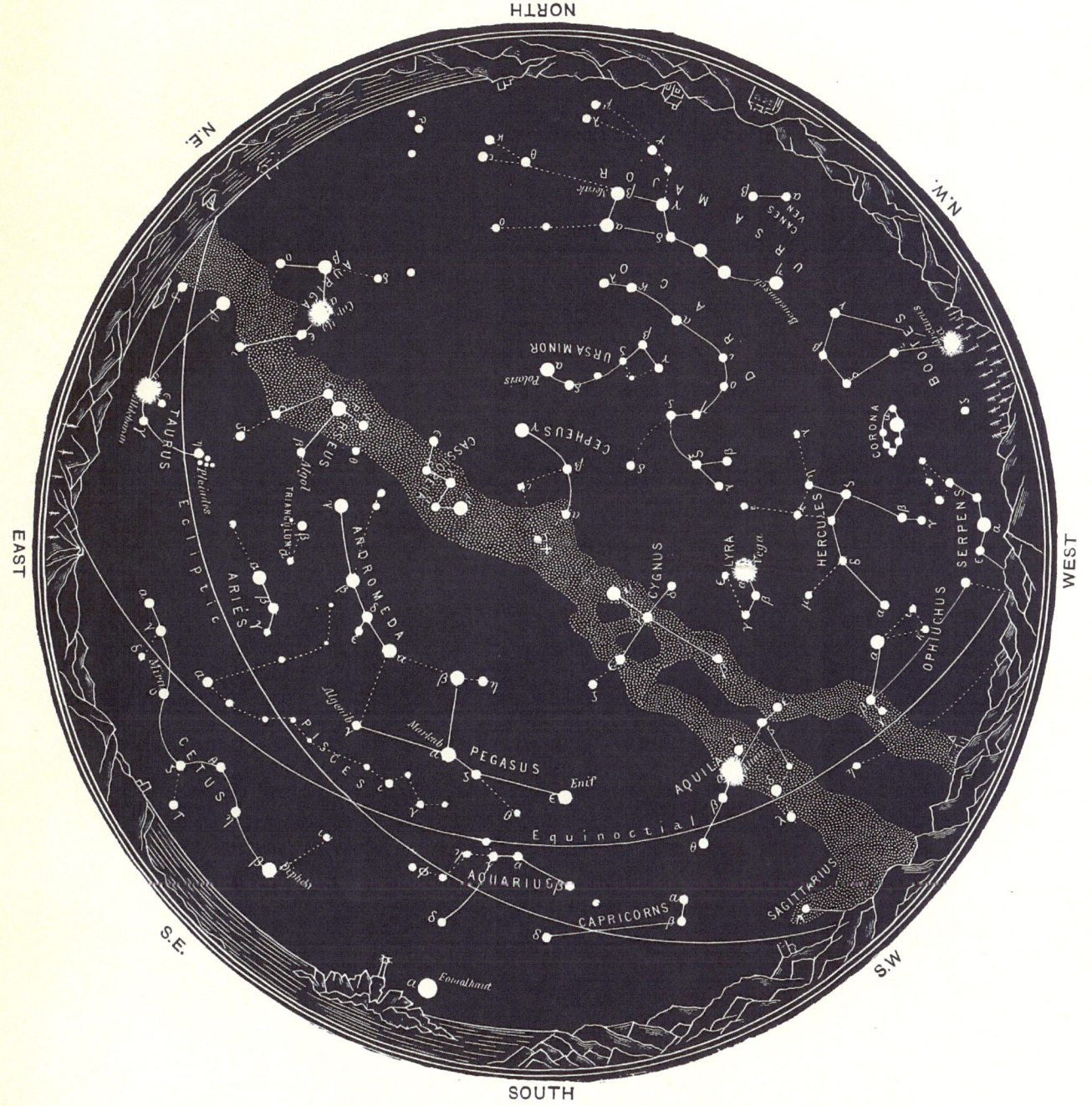

The above Map is a representation of the Starry Heavens in the Evening at the following Dates and Hours:—

SEPTEMBER 11 at	...	... 10.40	OCTOBER 1 at	...	... 9.20	OCTOBER 21 at	...	... 8.0
26 ,,	...	... 10.20	6 ,,	...	... 9.0	26 ,,	...	... 7.40
21 ,,	...	... 10.0	11 ,,	...	... 8.40	31 ,,	...	... 7.20
26 ,,	...	... 9.40	16 ,,	...	... 8.20	NOVEMBER 6 ,,	...	... 7.0

The circular boundary of this Map represents the Horizon, with the principal points of the compass indicated. The Cross in the centre is the zenith or that part of the sky which is directly overhead.

A list of Arabic names of the Principal Stars corresponding to the Greek letters in each Constellation is given on page 16.